THIS BOOK
BELONGS TO

The ALPHABUG BULLY BUSTERS

by Jeryl Christmas

Illustrated by Kurt Jones

ACKNOWLEDGMENT

I would like to thank Mary Mallette Wood, who was the guidance counselor at Lesslie Elementary School, for giving me the idea to use the Alphabugs in addressing the serious issue of bullying.

Always be kind—
it's the right thing to do.
You never know
who may be looking at you.

Bullying's wrong—
don't ever take part
In hurting each other
or breaking a heart.

Caring for others
will make you feel good
When you follow your instincts
and do what you should.

Don't follow the crowd
if the crowd's doing wrong.
That road can be bumpy
and often too long.

Even the heart
of a bully would melt
If he were the victim
and saw how it felt.

Feelings of others
should be a concern.
That is a lesson
we all need to learn.

Goodness wins out
when we each take a stand
To empower those weaker
and give them a hand.

Harassment by bullies
with gossip or threats
Is cruel and unfair
to the one it upsets.

It often takes courage
to do the right thing
And ask an adult
for the help he can bring.

Just open your heart
giving others a chance
To hear the same music
and join in the dance.

Keep *doing to others*
as you'd have them do unto you.
That's a rule
which is golden and true.

Let's all be supportive
of those who do right.
Rally together,
but don't ever fight.

Many will stumble
and take the wrong road,
But you take the high one
and stay in that mode.

Never let others
influence your walk
If they like to bully
and use hurtful talk.

Often a bully
will try to attack
Or intimidate others
who cannot fight back.

Put feelings of others
ahead of your own.
What a difference that makes
when a kindness is shown.

Quit saying mean things
about others that hurt.
Dig deep to find good—
don't go digging up dirt.

Reach out to your neighbor
with arms open wide.
Your conscience will show you
and be there to guide.

Stop bullying
from being a problem today.
You be a leader
and show us the way.

Try starting a club,
group, or even a team
To be Bully Busters
and follow that dream.

Using your head
and walking away
From a bully is hard,
but you don't have to stay.

Villains need victims
in order to thrive.
Without them, their power
would never survive.

We all see the damage
that bullies can do
When they hurt those you love,
or even hurt you.

"**X**"-terminate bullying
right on the spot.
You know you can do it—
just give it a shot.

Your goal should be this,
and it works for us all:
Don't put others down
just to make you look tall.

Zero's the number
of bullies there'll be
If we follow the Alphabugs—
A to Z.

So pledge with these Alphabugs
here in a cluster:
I promise to "bee"
the **BEST BULLY BUSTER!**

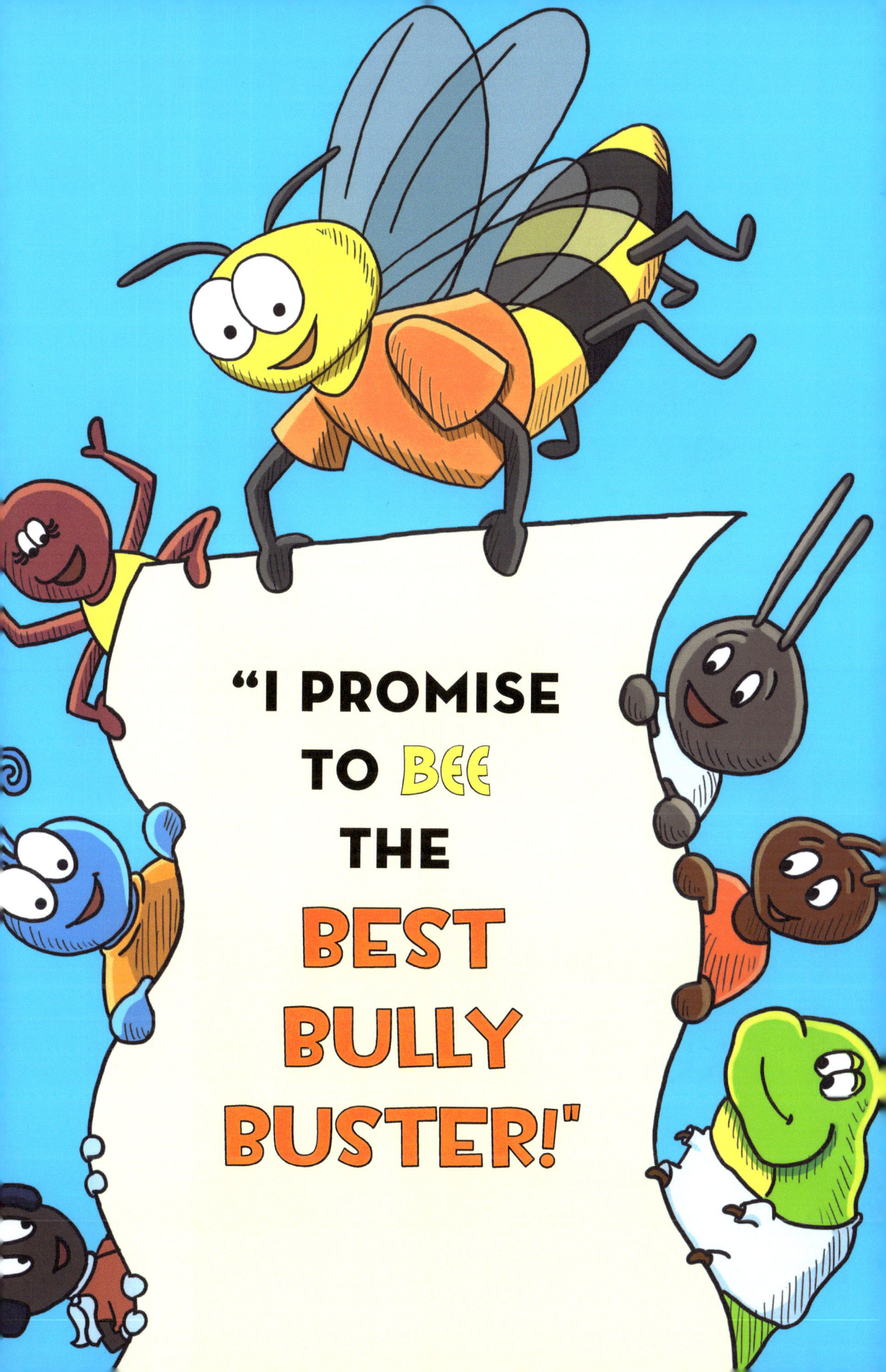

"I PROMISE TO BEE THE BEST BULLY BUSTER!"

ThE

Aa
Bb
Cc
Dd

Ee
Ff
Gg

Hh
Ii
Jj

Kk
Ll
Mm

ALPHABUGS!

Nn

Oo

Pp

Qq

Rr

Ss

Tt

Uu

Vv

Ww

Xx

Yy

Zz

The

End

www.ingramcontent.com/pod-product-compliance
Lightning Source LLC
Chambersburg PA
CBHW042109040426
42448CB00002B/193